Quote the Best Out of You

DR. UDO F. UFOMADU

© 2004 by Dr. Udo F. Ufomadu. All rights reserved.

Printed in the United States of America

No part of this publication may be reproduced, stored in a retrieval system, or transmitted in any way by any means—electronic, mechanical, photocopy, recording, or otherwise—without the prior permission of the copyright holder, except as provided by USA copyright law.

Scripture references are taken from the King James Version of the Bible.

Published by:
U C & P
P.O. Box 746
Selma, AL 36702-0746

ISBN 0-9754197-3-0
Library of Congress Catalog Card Number: 2004195407

Acknowledgements

To God be all glory. Thanks plentifully for using me.

~Udo

INTRODUCTION

My quotes are used in showing God's supremacy, in inspiring people, in teaching people to think analytically, in building teams and fostering unity, in managing wealth, and in instilling self-confidence in people.

These quotes are unique simply because they address the problems facing children, adults, communities, and organizations in today's world.

The quotations afford the reader an opportunity to heighten his or her personal self-esteem and elevate his or her organizational pride.

I have essentially used these quotes in telling stories, in answering questions, and in giving an individual or group a sense of direction.

The spiritual quotes compel an individual to unlock the rusted lock blocking his or her growth. The majority of the quotes motivate an individual to recharge his self-confidence and boost up his achievement level.

A reasonable mastery of the quotations will even persuade one to take a hard look at what "success" really means and encourages him to see the degree of success already attained in his/her life.

Many times have we spent time and energy worrying about the one percent insufficiency in our lives instead of expending such energy in thanking God for the ninety-nine percent sufficiency evident in our lives.

We have the audacity to grade our lives. If you let the devil grade your life, he will appropriate a larger percent to your struggle. Sometimes, the struggles that we give credit to the devil are actually God using a particular situation to prepare us for the better life ahead of us. I have experienced these situations many times, and it's continuous so I know exactly what I'm talking about. I don't let anybody or devil rank me at any stage of my life. I grade myself. That's why I can categorically boast in the Lord whenever I choose.

If you continue to let the devil grade you, he will continue to magnify your insufficiency. But if you learn to grade yourself with my motivational quotes, you will uncover how to develop enough personal power and eliminate self-defeating methods that suffocate unity, love, joy, peace, and growth.

When the appointed time for materialization arrived,
Your difference was not even in consideration for the actualization and materialization
of that person, before formation, God called legendary.

If the problem you are trying to solve refuses to adjust,
You may have to adjust your own self.

Certain for David, a favorite
His gratefulness his glory.
Certain for Goliath, the vain
His pride, his collapse.

There will always be a problem to solve, for
life is made to be challenging.

To a liquor manufacturer
Has a seed reached out to harm
A liver so needed
Being unfair to a gift.

Your faith worked out a pride
As indecision was utterly defied.

Even "procrastination" and "frustration"
were disgraced.
When prayer conquered, when prayer
displaced.
The preamble of glory is what we've seen so
far
For your best is yet to unload

The devil's obstructive machine
Will never deter a success of a planned price

Your faith in God and your belief in
forgiveness,
Have cleaned all negative buildups, giving
way for prosperity to suffice

Many times has the devil approached me
with worn out techniques and secrets that
the Holy Spirit has already leaked.

Hoping and believing
you pray a lot
Procuring and acquiring,
your faith is hot

If wishes alone guarantee success,
Everybody, then, is a success

A great player covers the mistake
Of a fellow player during a game
But talks it over after the game
Or forgives and forgets about it.

I feel successful when God is happy, when I am happy, and when my family is happy.

The Ten Commandments is the ultimate instrument for assessing morality norm.

Success is not tied to luck; It is tied to a promise to those who diligently Work hard and seek good.

The mastery of relationship with the Owner of everything that I want should come first before the mastery of everything that He owns.

The God of North America is the God of West Africa; Their harvests are only dependent upon their seeds, time, and soil.

Be careful whom you elect or choose
as a leader, husband, or manager. For
a purposeless leader directs a
purposeless flock.

Business plan, HAACP plan,
personal plan
Are essential navigation tools.

Since I have learned to pray, plan,
and wait
for the real Master Planner to
initiate the plan, then have I
harvested more than enough and ate
plenty good through and beyond
expected span.

God, the Master Planner, has not failed us yet.

The devil may hate you with a passion.
But you can make him respect you with an action.

If you appreciate a person, he or she will increase in performance.

The Bible is the only reasonable compass for sailing the know-not.

Wisdom without the fear of God is a dangerous wisdom.

Give your treasured employees, partners, or clients what they cannot find elsewhere and they will remain with you.

A wealth of experience awaits you, if you start at the bottom and grow to the top.

Success without God is on the surface.

A success without the word of God is a sure mess.

Revenge thou not
With a cheaper shot.

Tell not your problems to the people
who cannot solve it or pray
genuinely about it.

I am the one that is thirsty,
I am the one that must look for pure
water.

We can hope the same way David
hoped when he picked up the sling
and stone to face Goliath.

Let not a junk immaterialism
paralyze
God's favor already delegated to
patronize.

Avoid any that's so untrue,
Believe in yourself
As success unwraps itself.

A person that cares
is
A person of the people.

You can never become a positive if
you
Hear, touch, and meditate in
negative.

Not everybody or everything sent to
you is designed for your goodness.
The devil sends some things too.

It is never too late
To achieve and realize
The dreams, goals that await
Attempt, rather than to analyze.

If you show me your mentor/role
model,
I will show you what you are likely
to become.

A good manager is
That coach who knows how
To get players to play
Together for one purpose.

He that encourages and teaches
others,
Encourages and teaches himself too.

Success avenges thy cause.

God formed you to dominate
An awkward, slippery world
That justifies atrocities, injustices
That even great people settle for a
compromise.

What you expose your eyes, brain,
and ears to
Determine what you seek after and
consequently become.

Let your plans be meaningful,
Moreover, let your goals be
attainable.

For you to find something,
You've got to look for it.

Your level of obedience
Determines your level of
procurement.

Like a beautiful flower
You can blossom
Blossom as a rising star and will
shine
Shine more than the brightest stars.

I am going by what God Knew
before I was formed
I am not trying to prove anything

Success is designed, arranged, and
mapped for them
They that will listen to their parents
Parents that will instill values, take
them to a good church
Church that teaches respect for God,
life and authority.

Love good over malevolence,
Peace and goodness you must like,
Like a beautiful flower,
I know you can blossom.

You may not find what
You are looking for the first time

Because God, the Commander, has
Not disappointed us yet, we must
continue
To trust and obey

Not knowing all the answers to my
concerns
The succor of the Omniscient was
solicited
And He comforted with Psalms 27:1,
Psalms 118:6, Jeremiah 17:5-9,
Isaiah 26:4, & Isaiah 41: 10-13.

Her faith fiercely maximized in the
right
Capacity, she unequivocally knew
that if she may
Touch His cloth; she'd be free of her
plight

Your plan and dreams are valueless
Until you implement them.

Always add God to any package
Designated for your children.

The value of your business
Appreciates each time you honestly
Involve God and His principles

Abraham, David, and yourself
Know how bright
It glows when maximized faith turns
darkness to daylight,
That enemies and head enemy when
defeated
Resort to flight.

How you do it
Is as important as
How you say it

Faith in God, I have exhibited when I
fight
Some battles, yet I crave for faith
activated in a way
That all my Goliaths vamoose at my
sling's sight.

Starting: it is the only remedy.

And now my good God, reigning
from the greatest height
Show me how to activate, maximize
my faith, I pray
So at all times, I'll be one
unquenchable, indomitable light.

Your ability should never be
Overshadowed by your inability

You may not be the first to
Think of an idea, but you
May be the first to reap the result
Of putting the idea to action

Your mistakes are regrettable only
If nothing is learnt from it.

To me, a present abode
Is just a palace,
An abode to come is simply a bigger
palace.

What ever you call yourself
Is what you really are.

To me a present ride is super,
A ride to come
Is simply a better ride.

Climbing to the top is natural
But flying to the top is unnatural
For wingless creatures.

Real knockout occurs
When you cannot get up again.

To me my family is the best,
A family that fears God
Is simply number one.

Doing what makes you happy
Defines your degree of success

To me, my present job is good,
A job to come
Is simply a better job.

How you see it matters less
All I see is enough and excess

To me, I'm just as wealthy
A wealth to come
Is simply an addition

Successful parents instill value
By living the value

"Forwardever" is now a stand
nothing will invade

To me, I'm just as healthy,
A health to come
Is a better health.

"Was" is the past tense of "is".
If you discover that "was" is not
suitable for the sentence
Don't be afraid to use "is".

Let your ambition
Be on a mission
Faith-backed goals meet your
definition
As you embark on a success
expedition.

Be aware that discouragement serves
prohibition.
Know ye that criticism feeds an
inhibition.

Activated confidence and intuition
Will generate a strong acquisition
And diligently attract a coalition
Of honorable and heavenly
intervention.

If you know what you
Are looking for, you'll find
What you are looking for.

People strive to be better
When you encourage their effort.

Just peeping through the windows of your heart
I saw the insecurity clouding your eyes
Struggling not to fall apart,
Still you ordinarily fell to rise.

Never let
A bad season
Overshadow
A good season

Nothing is more fulfilling
Than doing what the devil thought
I couldn't do

I know a way out of this pain
Through a God of mercy and love
Waiting and willing to regain
The control of a flier capable as a dove.

The only step I see in front of me is
more than enough.

Achievers always say, " We will try"
And not, "We cannot".

I still reminisce on the last push
Cutting through a deadly ambush
With God, The Master Planner, in the lead
We cut, we fixed, and we reevaluated in full speed.

Why settle for good when best is nigh.

If you keep pretending to be
You'll become.

You are programmed to succeed,
Your little light is still on,
Quench it never.

The first step to solving
A problem is finding out
What the problem is.

The Sauls are running
They head for a change, I hope
The Davids are awake
They head for a victory celebration, I know.

The time it takes pretending to conform
Is the same time it will take to conform.
You might as well conform to the norms of the hopeful.

Goals are now attainable
Even in a packed session of doubters

You can get it
But you must persist
To get it at last

Everybody's ideas are needed
Until they are no longer needed.

For all, the stream of happiness
flows
To all the wind of gladness blows
Your choices and your actions make
the difference.

There is an Omniscient Consultant
that the ordinary can always share
With the well-to-do & the affluent
group of his/her community;
God is available to all.

If you desire to make your vision
plain
Make it plain and be happy.

Needless for a man-made god since
The God I serve provides all my
needs

If your Christian music
Nourishes your soul,
Nourish you own soul please.

If celebrating in the Lord
Boosts your spirituality,
Boost your spirituality please.

Do not depend on people
To make you happy
Because those people may be
unhappy.

If happy gatherings
Satisfy your soul,
Then satisfy your soul.

Remember that your present
Level is a promotion for someone
else.

Do not spend all your life
Waiting for someone to advance you.
Promote everything about
Yourself with the wisdom of God.

Wait for no human
To better your life.

Ask questions if you must,
But shut up if you lack
Knowledge on the subject matter
being addressed.

Wait for no mortal
Look for positive avenues.

It is better to be a good listener
Than to be considered a foolish talker.

Wait for no mortal
Look for positive avenues.

A friend or relative when things are good,
Should be a friend or relative when things are bad.

Wait for no special rationale
To make yourself happy

Wait and have no doubt
But don't stop praying about it.

Wait no more for their clout,
Have faith and take worthy chance.

Blessed are those who go out of their way
To lessen others burdens.

Wait no longer for your difference to discourage
Turn your uniqueness to assets for all circumstances.

Give your employer what s/he
Cannot find in someone else and
He will retain you.

Any level of job or education is
better
Than having none.

With the Omniscient in our corner to
provide
We have got it made

What you teach your children
Is what they will teach your
grandchildren

Have you ever thought about
Taking your hobby to the next level?

The portion of your life that you
delegate to the devil
Is the portion that he will work with.

With the Omniscient on the lead to
guide
Our conquest has stayed.

A new reaction induces
A new acquisition.

With the Omnipresent now firm on
our side
We are confident and unafraid.

If you want new things
Try new things

Backwardness turned a human into a pillar of salt
Looking back endangered and put a travel on a halt.

I'm back because you were reliable the last time.

You have to love something to be good at it.

Playing back kept a loser down
Forward march won the winner a
crown.

Some felt I wasn't fit
God called me a perfect fit.

A winner is that individual who
Knows how to fall and get back up,
How to try new things,
And how to persist in good faith.

Some said I couldn't
God said I could.

An effective leader or manager
Learns   what to do, Listens on how
to do it,
And helps everybody do it better.

God will reach out to you
The same way you reach out to
others.

When tears of sadness
Strolled down
My cheek constantly,
God comforted me immensely.

Wise people know when to tell God
And when to tell man.

When wickedness encompassed
Me for a kill
God lifted me.

When some doubted your capability
God believed in you.

Successful people are not afraid of making mistakes
Rather they avoid making the same mistakes
Over and over.

The Lord is my supplier
There is no rationale for nonsense stress.

When you think hope is gone
God reassures you authoritatively.

Always strive to be better than
Your role model.

If you want to be a leader,
Be willing to learn and be willing to teach,
And be willing to practice what you teach.

How you present yourself
Is how you'll be perceived.

When some saw my cup empty
God called it running over.

The Lord is on our side
No wonder we were certain and so sure
Of quenching our thirst with water so pure.

The devil and apostles used to
encircle us
They used to enwreathe us about
But in the name of the Lord
Almighty Father, we have banjaxed,
Stonkered, and scuttled them all.

For a time, darkness looked on
Suddenly, "Cock-a-doodle-doo," a
rooster crowed
Darkness disappeared
And I knew it was my morning
Directing all kinds of fish to my net.

Look beyond a bad past
Strive for a better tomorrow.

Avoid jealousy
A source of hate.

Let peace be a badge
Wear it at home
In the city,
In the field,
And when you travel.

Thou hast become your own enemy,
Thou hast doubted the potential
Of a tree planted by the riverside.

Now sanguine about my own harvest
I comprehend the sum of what my
eyes saw not
About gifts,
I comprehend the total of what many
ears hear not
On gifts,
Just give another
and another will bless you.

It is not about how fast the food is
cooked,
But how well it is cooked

Great players create opportunities,
Wise people take worthy chances.

Speak less when you are angry,
For an angry person is not a reliable
person.

A tree with sense gives fruit to
another
And receives abundant rain and sun
from another.

A cent or dollar gift to a reliable
charity,
A gift so genuine in a worldly stage
where
Abundance chases wise actors who
Outperform actors who have not
comprehended yet.

I wrote my blessings down this
morning
And I was amazed at all the things
that God did for me.

I tried a new thing
I got a new result.

If your friends' actions
Are repugnant to moral justice
Be careful.

If your friends' actions
Are insensitive to others pain
Leave them alone.

You thought you were in bad
Shape until you met people
In worse shape.

You are not a failure simply because
you got back up.

If your friends actions
Disobey authority
Avoid them.

If you want to change your group,
Start by changing yourself.

The courage you need most
Is the courage to start.

If their actions
Encourage education
Hold 'em tight.

Why should someone else believe
In you when you doubt yourself
constantly.

If his or her action thinks
Bad drugs are cool
Call him or her a fool.

The energy expended worrying about
What you have not
Could be spent rejoicing for what
You have.

If their actions
Discourage love for others
Be careful with them.

Success can only be defined
By you.

I want to improve on my character
Before improving on my reputation
because God is interested in my
character but my ego is interested in
my reputation.

If God and family
Are meaningless to your associates,
Reevaluate your association.

If their actions seem hopeless
Run away, runaway baby.

It is just nice to be nice.

Life is like a game
You are the referee of your life
Your life is controlled by each
Whistle you blow.

If thinking by itself makes
A winner, then everybody is
A winner because we all think.

Think positively and execute
Your positive thoughts.

God, a source for any resource, I believe
Supplies all your needs, if you believe.

If your problems go home with you
All the time, your home will have problems
All the time.

To a society, you may be just a man
But to your group or your family
You are a king for the things
You supply and things you manage.

In all educational build-up and
In all academic pile-up
Harmonize it with a degree in
wisdom/understanding
From the University of Heaven
In manifestation of a super force for
All realms.

Love progresses but enmity
retrogresses.

What worked for Mr. And Mrs. A
and made them happy
May not work for Mr. And Mrs. Z.

Learning from your mistakes
The devil has paid double
For the pain and all the trouble.

A pretty morning has come, fully loaded
With a unique and special kind of upgrade.

In pursuit of a God endorsed goal,
they will criticize,
But let not their criticism occupy a
space in your mind
For that same group that called you
strange will call you amazing if your
effort pays off.

The birds are singing about my
morning,
The Davids are already dancing
about my morning,
My morning is plain and self-
explanatory,
A morning with love, joy, and full of
glory.

You can drink
From the fountain of uniqueness
You can swim
In the ocean of happiness.

If they did not love you when you were bad
And still don't love you now that you have changed,
They probably have a problem with your creator.

If praising God makes the devil mad
But gives you control,
Make him mad and take control.

If raising your hands to the almighty
Offends Satan,
Offend Satan.

If going to church bothers some folks
Bother those folks.

It is honorable to have credit
But it is dishonorable to live on credit.

Food always on the table
A sign of God who is able.

If valuing positive diversity provokes
Be proud it provokes.

If losing weight enhances your self-esteem
Enhance your self-esteem.

The overestimation of the iniquitous energy
Is the underestimation of the positive energy.

If showing love makes you feel
supreme
Feel supreme.

In God's training camp
Less came as a training technique,
Abundance followed as a tool,
Sharpened by Heaven to overrule.

A roof over our head
Confirmation of what God said.

In thy going out,
You wear a princely emblem
In thy coming in,
You declare the glory of God.

Uneasy plans schemed to curtail you
Weakened.

The only way to start becoming what
you aspire
Is to start becoming.

Ammunition maximized to derail
you
Zeroed out.

Efforts strategized to keep you down
Head for disintegration.

Seeds of faith in germinating stages
Draw unfriendly attention.

Your river gradually turning to blue
oceans with varieties therein
Awakes the devil's fear.

The only solution to attacking a problem
Is to start attacking the problem.

Faith now activated
Marches you forward and forward
Toward a reward
For those seeds gallantly sown
In a fertile soil.

During the day, thou coruscates,
Under the sun, you flash
At nighttime, thou glares
Under moonlight, you glitter.

Nothing will occur
Until you make it occur.

Winners use adversity
To their own advantage.

The way your business treats your clients,
And cater to their needs
Determine your share of the community's economic harvests.

In spite of a sick body and large crowd,
She tried
To touch the hem of Jesus' garment.

Despite size and incredible weapon,
He tried
To annihilate Goliath with a slingshot.

Even though Zacheus was invisible
in a crowd,
He tried
To lay eyes on Jesus, by climbing a
tree.

You may not enter an Ivy League
college
But you're in a college.

You may not pray like the reverend
prays
But you communicate with God.

You may not be able to write like
Shakespeare
But you expressed your thoughts.

You may not be able to sing like him
or her
But you sing

You may not be able to teach like
Jesus
But you share ideas.

Time for planning
Is different from time for execution.

People are attracted to ideologies
That solve their problems.

In a fish dominated ocean,
A woebegone fished only wood.

In a world of uncertainty
A defeatist prays not.

In a world of give and take
A forsaken only takes.

In a time of peace
A reckless fusses.

In a world where you don't know
Until you try
A downhearted tries not.

In a place where education is free
A disconsolate gets none.

In God's presence, your color
matters less
Even though he made color and no
rectifying.

In God's kingdom, your intelligence
is baseless
Because he authors wisdom and
understanding.

Like a wise antelope, I spotted the
lion and ran
I ran, ran, ran, towards a bright light
And the light rescued me
And made me wiser

In a time of upliftment
A dolt discourages.

In a world filled with beautiful
creations and colors
A pessimist says there's no God.

Each time the devil said that I
couldn't do it,
God said I could.

Spend more time on solutions
Than on problems.

A better today I can describe vividly,
And try forgetting yesterday
Which is unworthy of my sadness.

Created children of the world are dying,
Identified children degrade immeasurably,
And we search for unidentified flying objects.

Those who doubt your ability directly
Doubt the ability of your God directly.

There is a reward for everything
done well.

The person who is still hesitant to
give
Has not read Luke 6:38, Proverbs
19:17 and Acts 20:35.

There is no value to your dream
Until you act on it.

As the anticipated time draws near,
The iniquitous energy looks silly,
Controlling and feasting on fear,
A wise person plants in the summer,
fall, even when chilly
A good person blossoms incredibly
without tear.

Let not your knockdown
Be a knockout.

The value of faith appreciates
Each time you act upon it.

My obligations and portions have I
kept,
Love and respect have I given,
Confident that a prayer has swept
All competition in a match so power
driven
That an ego bled and all pride wept.

A Christian that treats the poor with
cruelty has not read Proverbs 17:5 or
Proverbs 21:13.

Channel your frustration
To positive action.

Super leaders consider everybody's
suggestion
Until the suggestions are no longer
needed.

But I know come tomorrow,
With our plan directed by heaven,
We'll laugh; we'll praise,
And we'll sip on ice water.

Your faith and hope paid off,
Your good desire quenches not,
Your dreams suffer not, your loaded
ship just blasted off.

If you are mean to the poor,
Proverbs 14:21 questions your
Christianity.

In that pleasing world that I hanker
for,
A rich shares wealth as commoners
ditch,
Poverty in a bottomless pit without
ground,
As hope and happiness in all faces
found.

In a world that I desire
Good speech works to alleviate pain
and outreach
To all needs, that is enough crowned.
Satisfaction for all is then year
round.

You trash Proverb 21:13
When you mistreat the poor.

How can the door open
When you have not knocked?

In a beautiful world I yearn for
Each constantly explores a way to
reach another's need
So selfishness is bound.
Sharing becomes a duty as harvest
abound.

Why tell everybody what you are
planning to do
When everybody will eventually find
out
When you are done.

The greatest quote of all is: "God
loves you."

What you call snack, may be
somebody's dinner elsewhere.
Something to think about.

To heaven have I looked up for aid,
A sigh of relief each time heaven said,
" It is alright."

Sometimes it takes longer than I expected,
But in all, goodness and mercy I collected.

The good of the talks are all I hear,
For the bad of the talks instigate a fear.

You may get more if you are
appreciative and thankful
For the one you already received.

If you are able to do it one time
You'll be able to do it all the time.

You may not be able to cook the
delicacies like her
But you can at least boil water for
her.

It takes one additional penny to make
99 cents a dollar,
Every penny is important.

Selective listening makes peace the way
For love and self-aggrandizement to stay.

God's way
Is the only way out of this mess.

There is something to gain
When you learn to work with people
positively different from you.

When the blind worked together with
the deaf
As a team,
All written information to them was
read perfectly
And all the voice information was
heard perfectly.

Combine your strengths
And you will make a difference.

Encircle by the Holy Ghost,
A sudden attack,
Deterred,
A planned attack,
Marred,
A victory celebration planned.

Fresh energy and assurance are
stirred,
To soar me to the greatest altitude.

Kindness well learned and inherited,
If misinterpreted as weakness,
So be it and let it be.

Where God's umbrella folds not,
Is where I want to sit.

It is very biblical to be
Sensitive to others pain and need.

Where everyone can do all things
through Christ
Is what we have to build.

Be not upset when a person asks you
to repeat what you said,
Because that person may have
admired the way you just said it.

Where size, looks, age, color, origin
matters not
Is where love lives.

Laugh not at anyone who cannot
effectively do what you do
Because you may not effectively do
what he/she does.

Anytime you
Or your business
Is adaptive to others culture,
You are bound to gain
Cooperation from such culture.

Where grace abounds
Is where I want to be.

Where God's mercy endureth
Is where I take shelter.

It is progressive to separate
someone's offense
From his/her cultural background.

Always strive to be a good example
No matter what position you hold in
a group setting.

Where God's riches supply needs
Is where I stand.

A great leader acknowledges that
A person's difference can actually
mean his or her strength to the team.

Where peacemakers are called God's
children
Is where I belong.

Where envy is not sin
Is where I forbid.

Everybody is responsible for what goes on in a business or group setting.

God's law on mistreatment should Override national laws on mistreatment.

God's law that you don't know May be hurting you.

Where the merciful obtain mercy
Is where I cherish.

A wise manager or supervisor
Considers his/her workers as team members
And not as unfortunate subordinates.

Some managers or heads consider themselves as team leaders
And not as superiors.

Bear in mind that behavioral
standards are not universal
What is accepted in South America
may not be accepted in South Africa.

Why laugh at the way someone tries
to speak your language
When you cannot even say that
person's name right.

Even Pele and Michael Jordan
Took advice from their coaches.

World covenant has not been kept
Peace forgotten and utterly forsaken
We ponder, we wonder, we wept
For gross selfishness, and bitterness,
is awaken.

If you obey Jesus' commands
He considers you a friend.

It's fulfilling to observe the inspiring
rectitude
Of these angels sent to my house.

The only way that you can teach a subject
Is to learn the subject first.

Harvest abounds
In every appreciative barn.

Only wise people
Accumulate in drought.

Teachers are still teaching,
Preachers are still preaching,
Mentors are still mentoring,
Water abound in quantity and in
quality,
Yet the fool is thirsty.

We may not know exactly what path
God leads us next
Precisely, all I see is abundance.

We may not comprehend a favor's
release or retention
Accurately, all I feel is goodness.

I am the best individual
To explain my relationship with
God.

Gratefulness,
An emblem,
Worthy to be worn,
Rain or shine.

All successful people have the same
things in common:
Perseverance, hard work, belief in
God, belief in self, and love for what
they do.

As a devil watches helplessly,
Battles led by General God
Are successful in entirety.
Walls are falling,
My Goliaths are fallen,
To rise no more.

To a tobacco company
Has his seeds gone to,
Deteriorating a lung so needed,
Being unfair with a gift.

Focusing on no good but negatives,
Desisting from calling myself
blessed
To please you and your ego,
Is disrelishing to heavenly justice.

Wait for no man
To boost your spirit.

That bad habit that you refused to get
rid of
Will eventually get rid of you.

A shoe too big or too small for your
feet affects your walk.

If that relationship
is not meant for you,
Stay away or it will affect your walk.

By your standard and measurement
I may not have enough yet,
But I sure know what and whom I
have
And I'm persuaded that he is able to
move me above, across, and beyond.

Habits that waited to devour have
vanished,
to darkness they're faded,
and into brightness deliverance
packages
await patiently.

An alcohol drinking has been
pressured by heaven
It has taken to its heel
It has gone into the dark.

Now wipe tears, weep no more,
A plagued land is about to laugh,
Unstoppable rain has been ordered,
For Jah has decreed good news.

Evaluate me not by yesterday's
mistake,
But by today and tomorrow's
greatness.

Giving in to the enemy is dangerous
But genuine defense is no bad
indication.

If it appears no door is opening
Wait and have patience
With prayers in charge
A double door will open
As choice fights for a chance
Select you the best
From two so blessed
Celebrate a conquest
With a praise so impressed.

I desire to enter all promised lands
I pray
To go and be of great service
To all You delegate me day by day.

I plan to unplan
if it is not God's perfect will.

Encompass and mold me like Jesus
Whose style and walk made a way,
For the ordinary creature to have a voice
In a kingdom that presents a pay and a choice
Equally to all princes and princesses.

Exchange thou not peace, love for detrimental tension
And rough times that embrace days and nights or wartime craze
And let peace and love be the theme for your convention.

An association that lacks morality
Lacks substance

An ultimate guide,
An ultimate directive,
An ultimate regulation,
An ultimate advisor,
An ultimate instructor,
A handbook,
A bible.

Worry thee less about criticism
And give decreased attention to war
But if pushed too far,
Drop all ammunition, pray and praise
Intensively like Paul and Silas
To attract a heavenly intervention.

N4 = RP (Necessary 4 = Rounded Personality)
God + Family + Church + School = Rounded Personality.

Care ye less about temporarily looking stupid at their speculation
For beloved Mary, Jesus' mother looked stupid those days as a pregnant virgin.
Thank God for divine conception.

I am always happy to be happy.

It is not biblical to love others more
than your spouse/ children or family

It is biblical to love others as you
love yourself.

Let peace and love manifest your
sophistication this season,
And let all ill concern fade and phase
away into the dark
And leave wars to the Master of
apprehension.

May be hard to forget
But we must forgive and forget
Forgiveness, a key to heaven's door
Forgetting, a balm for war sore.

Even though Sushi is good
I have not craved for Sushi,
Because I have not tried Sushi.

Love you positively,
Abhor you negativity
Show love, and be a blessing
And let's enjoy in harmony.

How better your works had become,
Your light will not flame out,
It has drawn might and strength.

Your pierced heart
Now fully healed
Has sealed your crushed bone
together.

How better your life had become for
a rematch and victory,
Your faith will not fade out
It has pulled a conqueror,
A lion of Judah.

Father, they doeth evil, we know
But only if thou alloweth them.

Selfishness and anger
abound here on earth
Father, who is Omnipresent, stand by
me.

Human beings are wingless
Because they are not meant to fly.

Thou standeth by me day and night
I will not fear.

The things God has done are
marvelous in our eyes.
Let the universe therefore look at us
and affirm that,
Forever Omnipresent Stands By You
(FOSBY).

Attack a status quo with patience,
persistence and progressive ideas.

She's of course a rounded CCL
Constantly scaring the devil to hell
A Classy Christian Lady
Will still be classy even at 80.

That individual that you hate and call
derogatory names today may be the
best individual to assist you
tomorrow.

She is so satisfied,
Need always supplied,
By God always magnified,
At all times, she praises,
For all things she prays.

There is no sense waiting to excel in
that,
Which is ungodly.

Good management is not only about
getting good workers.
It is also about getting good workers
to stay, work together and produce
quality output.

It is rewarding to be
Full of joy when in need
Full of glow when in plenty
Full of thanks in time of peace
Full of love in time of war.

People who are generally loved or
liked by other people,
Have love already occupying a space
in their heart.

She glows,
She knows,
Always sowing a good seed,
With abundant reaping guaranteed.

In inexpensive outfit,
She appears too legit,
In expensive attire
Can't help but admire.

You are not really ahead in a game
or a race
Until the final whistle is blown.

Even when quiet,
She epitomizes angelic sight
Confident and careful
Graceful and joyful.

You can help someone become smart
If you keep calling him or her smart.

Listen to all talks that your parents,
your pastors, your teachers, your
counselors, your supervisors, and
your prophets have to say.
May sound illogical
To you today, but will become
logical tomorrow.

She is classy and Godly
A combination so highly
Treasured for her heavenly traits of
sensibility, ability, and versatility.

Even when quiet
You epitomize an angelic sight
Confident and careful
Graceful and joyful.

Ask first for wisdom to handle
"enough"
So that "enough and excess" will not
blow your mind.

A child that obeys his or her parents
Will be obeyed by his or her children
when he or she becomes a parent.

A Christian mama is,
Firm but not mean,
Calm but not intimidated,
Tough but not rough,
Fanatical and so Pentecostal.

What degree of help and respect that
you accord your parents, supervisor,
pastor, or manager is the degree
you'll be accorded when your time
arrives.

Be not upset with one that sprays
saliva when speaking
Because he maybe having a malady.

A blatherskite without God
Is like a toothless bulldog.

A braggart or boastful talker without
God
Is a loquacious fool.

Faith, forgiveness, discipline, and
loving kindness is after all what
Christianity is all about.

Angels are sent to my house
Some are pretty and sagacious
Some are handsome and chivalrous
Each is fortified and prepared
All are equipped and fully loaded.

Baby
Starring at you constantly
No artificiality I see.

Please smile at my direction
Only if it is from your heart,
For a fake smile arouses my
curiosity.

Dignity and class override a fuss.

A silent response is so dignified
In a place peace is so glorified.

With a prayer in control,
Humiliate those deficiencies
That seem to bind.

To utterly believe
What you've not seen, is like
Placing a value, or a claim on what
is to come.

Thank you lord, for opening my eyes
wider to see love, not hate.

Take that crooked dollar
And give me a straight dime.

God, I thank you for broadening my
mind deeper,
Deeper to appreciate you more,
Deeper to put your first.

Lord, I cannot offer you a drink,
for thou drinketh not,
I cannot offer you food, for thou
eateth not,
So I am saying, "Thank you, sir."

One array of the rainbow is vibrant,
Together
All arrays are exciting, stimulating
And imposing.

Don't be nice to people only when
you want something from them.

I cried, like Solomon,
I cried for magnificent lead and guide,
With humility and no pride,
I receive the abundant wisdom supplied.

I'd rather be a small shot in a friendly environment
Than be a big shot in a hostile setting.

I stand, claim, and believe on today's wisdom and Receive,
Forthcoming wisdom expressed to Relieve,
The pain of some that still Grieve.

Love,
It does not constrain light,
It does not restrain growth,
It takes away envy,
It takes away bitterness.

Those businesses or ministries that you call "large and successful" used to be "small and doubtful."

It takes time
It takes faith
It takes perseverance to succeed.

Love,
It fertilizes your soil,
It organizes your seed,
It fuels your light constantly,
It nourishes your soul incessantly.

A team leader must be ready to
deliver all he promised his team for
achieving a particular goal.

It pays to be happy.

The ability to persist and not give up
is the secret to reaching our
destination.

Love,
It makes a way,
It brightens your future.

Love of God;
It gives you joy
It gives you peace.

Our importance is not based on what we accumulated, it is based on how many lives we impacted.

Success, in the highest order, Shows up when you think hope is gone.

The formula for success is "keep on trying".

If you expect premium,
You have to give premium.

Good things that last never come easy.
Hard work, and persistence, is the only way.

You don't necessarily have to be well known to make it in life:
Whatever it is you are doing,
Just do it well.

You are not successful if you are not happy.

Can we walk in unity and obedience
As in the time of Jericho
When unity and obedience broke barriers?

To your difference, I'll look beyond
To your positive uniqueness, will I embrace.

From whence cometh E. Coli's
enemy?
Not from Jupiter, but clean hands,
cloths, utter sanitation, and thorough
cooking.

Listeria Monocytogen,
Your hatred for adequately heated
food is no lie
As your dislike, for sanitary
conditions, is no fallacy.

I tried not to imagine
I only endeavor to reason
At the devil's lost chance
In heaven over ignorance.

I dig no more
For answers to my papa's
progressive actions
I now know for sure
That enmity retrogresses, but love
progresses.

The devil's fire burns incessantly
Yet no heat we feel.

The devil has slashed with a sword,
Still no blood we see.

As we worship and celebrate Jesus
May we represent what He
represents.
May we love all that Jesus loves;
Love, peace, and giving.

Creation, I know it is
Evolution, some think it is.

Am I not supposed to thank thee
plentifully before grumbling for
moon and star that I want.

Catechize no more on my negatives
Explore at large on my positives.

If you loathe the way she looks
Sorry, I can't help you
Because the sagacious lady is not yours
Of course, the chivalrous lady is virtuous.

It is disgusting
When you stack, and pile your visions
With no actions.

I cannot play instruments like
DavidSolomonKings
But I can make sounds of praise.

It is repugnant
When dreams are destroyed
By fear of mortal disapproval.

In the absence of worldly
connections
My praise and worship linked me to
greater connections.

You do not have to down grade
someone
In order to up grade yourself.

Where God's anointing shatters yoke
Is where I see.

It is not beauteous
When faith stands alone
Without works.

It is even an abomination
When good people diminish
for lack of courage
For that person who avoids making
mistakes also avoids
growing up in life
Spiritually, materially, and
physically
For that man or woman who has not
grown lately
Has not tried something new lately.

I believe in the inside beauty, but the
first thing your intending husband
sees is physical beauty.
So fix yourself to the best of your
ability.

It is unbiblical to say, " I love you"
without showing love through
Prayer, support, and sharing.

What you have made up your mind
to become
Is what you will actually become.

Just try

Success without the wisdom of God
is like a water tank with an invisible
leak.
When you wake up in the morning,
the water in your tank is gone and
you cannot tell why.

The road to Success Avenue is
narrow
But Success Avenue is wide.

Utterly blessed,
We adamantly refused to be stressed.

I will be grateful if you give me a
dime today.
I will be more grateful if you show
me how to make a dollar tomorrow.

A son that comes close to his wise
father
Ends up being wise.

A daughter that helps mama in the
kitchen all the time,
Ends up being a good cook.

A person that has a good relationship
with God
Acquireth favor.

If we make our parents happy
They will make us happy.

If we make God happy by being
obedient,
Then He will make us happy.

Encompass yourself with the individuals who want you to be successful.

Avoid all avoidables because Some people are worse than Judas; They'll betray you without asking for money.

The bible is the indispensable manual for motivation.

Motivate yourself adequately and
have meaningful success.

What goes into a child's head today
Helps mold him/her for tomorrow.

Buy what you can afford
And not what you cannot afford.

Obedience draws rewards.

Today's hand wash is tomorrow's savings on medical bills.

Exclude the unwanted & include the needed

Sharing transcends all aspects of love.

Happy employees produce happy results.

If you keep trying, you'll become.

Unhappy input produces unhappy output.

To be the best father or husband,
Is a leadership role in the highest

To be the best mother or wife
Is a management role of immense dignity

You cannot let the one percent insufficiency
Outshine the 99 percent sufficiency

The CEO of U C & P

Dr. Udo F. Ufomadu, Ph.D., is the founder and President of Ufomadu Consulting & Publishing (UC&P), a business consulting/publishing firm based in Selma, Alabama. The firm specializes in business planning and book publishing. He is the author of the highly acclaimed books, _Anthology of Inspiration_ and _How to Become Extremely Successful in Business Management, Personal Management, and Family Budget Planning._

Dr. Ufomadu has 13 years of experience as a Consumer Food Safety Protection Specialist working with business management in regulatory and inspection capacity for the state of Alabama. He reviews, monitors, and verifies food industries' procedures in HACCP/SSOP plans relative to consumer protection and safety.

He is trained and certified in handling diversity in the work place. He obtained a Ph.D. in Business Administration from Madison University, a Master of Science in Administration and Supervision from Alabama State University, additional Master courses in Personnel Management from Troy State, and a Bachelor of Science in Business Administration/Management from Troy State University. He also attended the College of the Redwoods.

Dr. Udo Ufomadu was inducted as a member of the Institute of Management Consultants (IMC) in 2002. He is a professional member of American Management Association (AMA) and a professional member of the

Institute of Food Technologists (IFT), and a professional member of the International Association of Conflict Management. He is also a member of Tabernacle of Praise Church in Selma.

Dr. Ufomadu, also a 2003 and a 2004 Editor's Choice Award (International Library of Poetry) winning inspirational poet, consults nationally and internationally.

To order additional copies of:

Quote the **Best** Out of You

Call 334-418-0088
Or please visit our website at
www.UfomaduConsulting.com

www.ingramcontent.com/pod-product-compliance
Lightning Source LLC
LaVergne TN
LVHW091549060526
838200LV00036B/762